TRAMMEL

Charlotte Newman was born in Surrey in 1986. She read English at Selwyn College, Cambridge and holds an MA with Distinction in Modern and Contemporary Literature from Birkbeck, University of London. She won the inaugural Sabotage Award for Best Poetry Pamphlet in 2013 and was featured in *The Salt Book of Younger Poets* in 2011.

After a brief stint indexing the entire back catalogue of *The Erotic Review*, she worked as a journalist and publicist for a leading family law firm, writing articles for national newspapers while also contributing freelance reviews to *The Observer*, *The New Statesman* and *Poetry Review*, among others; she was shortlisted for *The Scotsman's* Allen Wright Award for theatre criticism. Charlotte lives in London with her husband, the poet James Brookes, and works as a political communications consultant, specialising in healthcare. *Trammel* is her first full collection.

REVIEWS

'Newman calls for a "barbed", aberrational, totally un-prosaic expression, and the result is far from easy by electric.'

Sam Buchan-Watts, *The Poetry Review*

'An angry, allusive and highly literary debut … this is poetry that is at once personal and political, of the moment, yet offering sudden sublime passages of timeless beauty. A bright new voice for dark days.'

Alex Preston, *The Guardian*

ALSO BY CHARLOTTE NEWMAN

Selected Poems (Annexe, 2012; 12pp)

Trammel

Charlotte Newman

Penned in the Margins
LONDON

PUBLISHED BY PENNED IN THE MARGINS
Toynbee Studios, 28 Commercial Street, London E1 6AB
www.pennedinthemargins.co.uk

First published 2016
This edition 2017

Printed in the United Kingdom by Bell & Bain, Glasgow

ISBN
978-1-908058-39-3

CONTENTS

DISSENT

ACKNOWLEDGEMENTS

Thanks are due to the editors of the following publications in which some of these poems have appeared: *Asterism, Litmus Magazine, Polarity, Penning Perfumes, The Salt Book of Younger Poets*.

Further poems appeared in the pamphlet *Selected Poems* (Annexe, 2013), for which Nick Murray merits particular thanks.

Warm thanks are also due to Andrea Brady, Gerry Cambridge, Michael Hurley and the members of Pierian, Dorothy Lehane, Roddy Lumsden, Sophie Mayer, Fiona Sampson, Claire Trévien and Carol Watts for their encouragement and assistance.

Especial thanks to Freddie Cox for sharing war stories.

for Jamie

Trammel

I

DISOBEDIENCE

But who knows what she spoke to the darkness, alone, in the bitter watches of the night, when all her life seemed shrinking, and the walls of her bower closing in about her, a hutch to trammel some wild thing in?

JRR TOLKIEN

Body Politic

How hard does it hurt to shoot
yourself in the foot and fold

yourself Christ-like into his
care; full harmony working

for you, though you may shrink in
stature, in meat worthiness.

Cut yourself short to make curt
by candelight, the canon –

can you explain its songstress;
cup a mother to your ear

to hear her tears pentangle
her *lyke wake* dirge misfire in

target practice. All the blood
of the house of Saul, hope caul

cauterised democratic
recall and taken in your

mischief. Salt-rimmed sisters less
Spanish, the spindrift second;

blitz revenger's tragedy,
pound for pound less coined weighty,

purely sovereign, special.
Make no bones right about it.

Synovium, cytokines
means this killing no murder

at the lychgate, our Cromwell
hastens the collective end:

the permeability
of sacrifice, osmosis;

trigger perfect malfunction
cupidity, caritas —

impermanence of objects
and their masters of mistakes.

No ideas but in things and
Nuneaton; sustainable

footprints at Falkirk, Moray,
hard and fast memorial:

such is Gateshead; so grateful
to grind it carried over

the fray and fuss, feverish
favour editorial.

In Vitro Veritas

Did you know who laid the dining table
like origami, taking in the budget cuts
of structural empathy, of courts
herding their insides forward towards

a tipping point of sorts?
There are men, who every quincentennial
hour pull hysteria to the rack
and recklessly to account.

They invest and invoke return;
spend a pronoun for provoking
lust. A lost custom, cut from annals
of sex guides and folded in turn into

that cursory swan by the napkin ring.
They had fabulous beards way back.
Today they have fabulous beards but
are from the other side of the tracks.

All the worthy discipliners, disciplinaries:
airily canonical and handy with
emoticons, give up no ghosts, only
anatomical inaccuracies like acorns.

Something akin to Newfoundland.

Spermatozoa caged in angry swells. All
is well and good when hell throws out
an ice pick, thick with autoimmune

efficiencies. Keeping tilting up;
hip and archaeology. Beat down embrace
recompense; gird your dishevelments
when asked and don't spit, face:

they'll only spurn you with a crude
embittered net. It's as far as you can get:
shovelling gravel through a stent, a
glassy, grovelling smack of well intent.

All that Jazz

Duff credit card exact size of visor.
Nothing to see/hear save for the slattern
scurry of slutty children, neatly boxed
centre square; parental advisory
cusped by husbanded blinkers. The kids cling
to dad, judge in the High Court of Lahore,
whose credit doth abhor the things his kids
once wore. Much more like you, who, then unstoned,
fleshed Al-Jazeera hip-wise from our side;
your side mere forbidden fruit for the weird
men leering from the window the wrong side
of the car stuck stubborn in a non-pro-
verbial rut. Maximise the freedom
of uncovered eyes: turn flesh into hard pulp fact.

Skeffington's Irons

Cursive lettering for recursive disgrace. Death panels? Rape kits?
Quitter on Twitter or

hunting accident on Colbert, Rush Limbaugh's
fabulous unadorned insides.

Primordially, the condemned man or woman even would flaunt
                under wrist cuts
without either ether or salvage; only the yeoman stole the show.

The opposite of wracking guilt, Monica Lewinsky in a tiger suit.
Anne Askew ruined everything;

the woman had so many foibles she resented anaesthetic.
If laudanum shouts louder than reprimands,

who holds the keys to the ultimate fighting kingdom, the
World of Warcraft warrior

who clearly holds the cards?
Charging for evidentiary nonentities

who wouldn't believe her, the Scavenger's Daughter;
power over truth beauty.

Proof is pudding to us all in times of

slutdom. Ask Alice when madness

stretches limbs, answers quaver;
caveman fever in hope of Niagara,

its pinches second rote. A rope is
a cape crusader, and everyone loves a jaunty joint;

at willow to wisp, heartfelt hardcore,
always a desolate dance floor.

Lockshy

Mendicant mouths for its own
mend, he can't, this is
a coffee-stained key,
a smoky eye kisses his
luxury.

All along the bus shelter
eyes batten, keening into wards,
wine-stained chased chaste nights;
absinthe of usury, this is
usually a mourning measure;

please wait while we receive
white hot Messianics
making murders of you.
Sit tight: and please write
material mentions of the way you

carry your paper past
the pauper, on Maundy money
no less, no more of that, my Lord —
race, you, to the poor house
proper — little aids

a lascivious maid.
Might as well send us a

digging, swigging Barry MacSweeney's
Tourettes-headed toothbrush,
brush-stoking flames sex-feet high

inside the initial turnaround about
down there. The fenugreek sky fattens
the young one, the slattern in
H.E.R. (Human Error Resources)
resorts to his

second-hand violence
via words exchanged in a
back alley, allayed, getting laid-in,
matching his mints to her
minutes, his pay-through-the-waistband

epiphanies.
Scenting Sweeney's sweet leather
strap for crass
in hand, assenting its relevance
for modern readers,

soubriquet nightingales sweat
only show how far we've come,
gone down, de-perverted
certain plexus, in the meeting
at the nexus of the flesh,

her two-pronged matrix

circumspected over brunch
and laundering.
When smoke looks thin
she looks at him;

there's time, no, hears
winging, carry on
square by square mile carrion
winning, one whole ethos
of train door toss-hers,

cut-loose investment bankers
and cut-her-throat wincing
while all this time is his time
on his terms; when she turns her back
you Midas well touch.

The Bechdel Test Botticelli

Illustrious and glorious mistress,
let women learn from you!

They have their everyday vexations
in vanity, varied, and passions

made supple with delights
and menstrual devices.

Judith returns to Bethulia
unburdened, bearing olives,

her maidservant Abra
clasping a trammel

of neurological functions.
This is what dialogue looks like.

Circa Assyria, someone stole
the tent pegs to give to Jael,

taking the head of the general;
jugular periodically severed.

They don't speak, their tongues
supplanted with lax hands

on the back of the forehead.
This is what scripting should be.

One might say she should
take a scalp as a trophy

substitute for miserly apostrophes —
subservient sophistry,

convenient humanist exempla.
Counterpart, daresay,

for those animalistic and
diabolical lusts that trussed

her speakerly minutes
and gave them to co-stars;

philistine armies never know
how to hold their peace.

Muscle / Emotion

Coaxed angel, past musket.

Crying for smart gingerbread,
kill my fees for me.

Feel, say, a note of psalms
in these Lisztomanic episodes:

mine do. Freud's literal issue
with clitoral tissue, a hard mast,

a muster to failing. After living with
its musk for months it straddles sands;

everything that's feminine is a synonym
for its weaker parts, the savviness

of permanent assets. Wills and
trusts of sensory. The whole host's laboratory,

hold in frankincensical wonder
a future rife with chemical origins

like lipstick, my grandmother's
purse. Her hearse undid the

good work of tea nights;
rose caddies, gorse teddies and

irises in false bloom on settlement.

Swoon / Republic

My stories were restrained, diligent and cautious. For years, I remembered one of my sentences with particular pride. Reading it now, it shows everything that was wrong with how I covered the event:

They stood crying before the coffins of strangers, offering roses and tiger lilies to young women they never knew.

I turned the dead engineering students into sleeping beauties who received flowers from potential suitors.

I should have referred to the buildings they wouldn't design, the machines they wouldn't create and the products never imagined.

They weren't killed for being daughters or girlfriends, but because they were capable women in a male-dominated field.

I should have written that then.

SHELLEY PAGE, *THE OTTOWA CITIZEN*

Mark the books or the women:
many open to the smell of snuff wood
(as if they could)
divine an obligatory DT laboratory,
nosing the grist to the grindstone.

We won't "shout on the street"
so don't shoot simple logic.
Will you.

Be still my heart a hard organ
to be shaped by a vice and a virtuous chisel.
I am a consummate skiver and a father's wonder

how they came up with that.

Blame remedial violence;
abuse/antithesis/synthesis/ miscegenation
over-easy. Consider the mother.

Mediate your differences and defences will
follow. Did I say defences. I mean defenceless.
A mean defender of traditional rights to vice
and virtue only in deafening fearfulness:

remember to send her a pailful of ears,
prove Caesar's galley womanless.
Alea jacta est only in death
on maternity pay please can it cost us less.

Blue velvet, once vulvic emancipates
immediately. When to duck and dive is —
live — is chivalric code of conduct,
twice removed — cough — balloting garrotte.
Son of a gun all shiny, mine's his twisted rust,

stamped sawdust one swift guillotine the
sum of its media charts. Bleeding hearts
shed edges on file, tuck into grave men,
check doors are secured.

Once shots heard send child, autism optional.
Refund my evening it did, miss. Did I can I call you

a miss. Kill it in marriage or severance
pay up. You will.

Ville-Marie makes gun shiver, seem clichéd.
Lost Buddha, make god Shiva; last days
of disco. Into this fray of mind mourning
matters only for second amendments.

Star Chamber

Indiana holding namesakes
fixable and to account.

Heaving women heavy to the laws
of men, hot to the black letter.

A blacksmith has money and a little mirror,
so besmirch. Rather question language.

Snake, wax, bottle, bitter
in our catalogue of graces.

Vexation and a veritable
marketplace of religion.

Held it vulnerable
against the scaffold

filedriver torso,
thumbscrew methodology

the Agamemnon counterpart
in furs of Valencia.

On and under Ophelia, oh
grief has never looked so beautiful

or wet burning up in
iron cuffs, almost Florentine.

Friends are ornate
hearing freedoms squeezed

into entry positions, learning
the trades of their mark squarely.

Prynne, Burton and Bastwick
mocked the malt of elder men

flocking the summit
for sedition of holy orders

to wear the man's stigmata,
ungodly denouncement

of entity, listless bodily matter,
always in *camera stellata*.

Amuse as a Martyr

I

Turn insides real after the fact.
Ignorant swab missed absence

harkened screams ill fit
for purpose, speed on a winding

shale. The mouth is
an ulcered medium; altered

states let gynos preen with
candour. This one rings

a bolstered brethren, covers
his backs, knits hats

for formaldehyde children,
offers tax breaks, haematopoiesis.

What else to compare the leucotome,
its rifts milk Leninist insults;

Artemisia bucks her stance
against unwanted heads,

leaves a thin hour between
the whole navel nothing

nerved under bad lights
to lap at gentle pity.

II

Reneged, an improvement
on tent pegs. Mire and

admire, malcontent;
her alkaline thirst

mere refusal to hold down.
Carotid nut cracks a garrotte,

weaves its wares on empty
jurors, abjures cruelty, gaiety

equally. The haematologists
welcome filth, coronal

method; systems meet
at the familiar crux

and catapult sample
with example, full

shoulders, vain piety,
fingers blame into

molecular portions, easily
digested. Hang his head

from rafters, it augurs
ilk on daughters.

III

Communist slab
claims inclusive borders.

Y-incisive ends make
auto-immune deficient,

why can't she hold her sides
together, incipient bone

marrow, tending her
tides' eyes maleficent.

Harrow, Holofernes;
it's all in your nature

to observe. Chromatography
of repellents: blood is cherry

pink when daubed. Nails
wrack their mistress

neat and kind, swell histopathology
tells you, father, tacit

with learning, adverse
where you lean your leucocytes,

how hard it is to hit
the hand Baroque built.

Tea at Troy

For Polyxena

O sign away her many
faces. I've known stasis
bleaker still. Until
once weak, they took

it all; they called her father
bloody. Helled sway,
pure fissure of force —
no gold — so gold it caught

in their throats like rupture.
Past voyeurs outsmart your
intellect, unlace you
as a corset: a sex splayed

on a vestibule ceiling
like wax on the waning moon.
Even the vents are crossed.
Our fathers cost us nothing:

a handful of Theban teeth,
quite centred on the hole
of their honesty, enmetalled
as if prone.

The risk of this
amazes, fleeting citrus
suns; only one hand fits
the sanded glove.

Her body is mettle,
how is your mother's heart?
How fit to start
a war; it fits

its metal beats.
It smarts between its
floors. I don't share
you anymore.

Uneyed and guttered,
your honey spent as
rapture, wrong
below. One cunt

too many fixes little
and is often brittle
money. Its ardour of
orange breathing;

the teeth will re-bury
the dead as themselves —
blunt as wont to be —
and see their silage

culled and wasted.
Once, I preyed on
faces; aloud I heckled
strangers, races, teachers,

eyeless breaches orbit.
My mother sanctioned me
and saved sour honour
passing. Honey, those are

waves out-lapping
our son, my sublittoral
image. Fix us, bid us
pray, his sudden certain

heat. My ask, dear love,
is precious. Posthumous;
is terror strangely bent.
I meant, is heartless

mentioned? I sanctioned
men your breast. I broke your
throat on purpose, love; I
meant your mannered stress.

The Reform Act

Diverse abuses at the knuckle and bone,
so often bare from rapping.
Hung and hanging seats from the rotten boroughs,
dapples all; Earl Grey will please

himself. Too many to suck apples why not
give yourself over to dis-
enfranchisement. Your odyssey is spoken
like odd numbers; fuck with the

OCD of its owner; you ask, he tells
you. What if you lack the fat
on the body and still think seriousness
is key and consequential?

This is an exercise in over-coming:
not quite truth in ownership,
nor resigning to be ever thus: excised,
deuterocanonical

and scandalous fair. Fidelity always
to the notion of state; steel
workers steal and disciple the task in hand,
tend mandatory affairs.

Trochaic, ironically iambic,
lilts in its favour; owning
itself over again until... not really
anything. Matches unfought

until unions stepped in to save the day.
And what did they say? *Per se,*
it mattered? No girls, whose pay cuts us right quick
and sharpened, holy smoke run

for paying lives. Would you ever ask? Or hold
their names sacred like rust and
clasped on Rolex or cursed fornicated cut
raw for all its matchsticks rut

pure energy. For a hole in the mouth, why —
what would you? Unmask the face
full for its moving menacing martyrdom.
Would you ever fear its grip

tighten at the dreadlock heart, a root and branch
petition full whack in
constituency terms, hub and spoke model
fights its neighbours' diseases.

London strokes her certainties, openly hit
silken in her infantries —
who mastered phosphorus for workers' unction
after business sewed lips shut;

such firm unfunctioning levelling of sound
mind, metric opposition;
homework pushed into placement, proud history
lies. Protectorate protests

interregnum injustice, hoping against
mandate someone has turned on
the oxygen; constitution of an ox
and soul of a snake. Mistake

not the minister of justice, slake a thirst
of the people, legal aids
us all when times are tough and straitened, traitor
at the gates of the Bar course.

Madam, the majority of working men
still cannot vote, what hope is
there for you? A quill stub, the will of the half
subdued; a coup of conscience

under malaise, knights of the shire. Horses break
the classes, mark the chartists
of the uplands, wunderkinds, the black country
nerve to call this great again.

II

DISARMAMENT

If it were done when 'tis done, then 'twere well
It were done quickly. If the assassination
Could trammel up the consequence, and catch
With his surcease success; that but this blow
Might be the be-all and the end-all here,
But here, upon this bank and shoal of time,
We'd jump the life to come.

WILLIAM SHAKESPEARE, *MACBETH*, ACT 1 SCENE 7

Lip Service, or, *La Haine*

Kiss you, take your children.
Riotous though it is, this shit's not for kids.

La Haine is bloating through drive-in speakers, serenading '68
miasma, she and Humbert staring down the barrel of the same
animal gun, wincing.

I will cross you if you come over all drunk-like,
tarantella con dolcezza with your latest organ grinder.
Find Slovenia with your head full of black, black wine
— dim donkey piñata —
an industry of collagen in scapegoat *giallo*.

How can I follow the winters,
archangel of interns; doubting Thomas
and his motives. Intimate metastasis
intrigues the censor, his biting wounds
inwardly glow

and Venus infers her worth from a table.
Her onus, her offending isotopes,
eyes big as gum balls, swings rapidly,
a timeshare in blazing saddles and
neat little ellipticals.

I hope, I know as you do,

we'll settle kindly out of court;
— you form –*isms* like Christmas —
sweet Mary shares her sweat with an ostler,
a meek swearing cross to milk.

Beach

Ours is a charnel house, yours is a wreck.
Circumspect, your rig docks on a ripcord,
embellished by destruction manuals and hard
rock. Our temper senses reward, and
tends a terminal treasure.

Your Gettysburg was bleaker than ours;
their engineers commandeered the ego
trip, and flipped a bitter term. Our guitar
went missing on that third day,
so we sent you out there

pissing in the wind for several certain
hours. Our cars went down by that
same upended ship and we were
shafted. They built rafts to bridge
the River Kwai; we saw them

tie a bootlace counter clockwise round
the rafters, shed their disasters after tea.
Poor wounded soldiers more than
ersatz marines and mariners to sea view,
its orphan-making profanities,

its unholy cue. Scenes to stutter rejoinder,
to scupper Pasolini, his boys:

their fits and starts and night terrors.
He reaps and, ugly, sows,
makes peace with broken oars; their

theatre absurd, their carnival workings out.
Inherit pity for the souls of dogs
even, hot flotsam, jetsam basilica;
an ethos in question in ditch bent
futura: your mayoral gift sans serif,

glyphs misfit with comic sands.
Its seraphed calms disquiet
our western front, its ink black Bauhaus
subjoins a bold oblique of font. Come speak
of flannel farms, of milk and eggs

midweek, of neighbours oddly sheltered.
Omaha's red, onerous roster
a carnage to commend thy spirit;
add in its violins, Jamaica Inns, restring
Stravinsky for riots of spring.

Trained Sleepers

Found Drowned BY GEORGE FREDERICK WATTS; OIL ON CANVAS, C. 1850
Miss Georgina Treherne BY GEORGE FREDERICK WATTS; OIL ON CANVAS, C. 1856

Stroke down, divide. Tilt, close ear clasp, cleaving lace-wards;
add dress, two different, heedfully vestal. Marginless, the other
       separating vertex
frames her twice, seamed red against a seeming winding sheet.
Raise maybe an eye, maybe a lid; cling onto
the two imagined driftwood slats, the dead-men's-fingers;
or fashion short thrift for her — for banked Ophelia —
supine, raised up waterly; she who shirks adjectives for lying flat-
       out
appeases her actuality, batten-eyed on the opposite wall.

Well done, well voided. Well welded-onto
and into, as if this were a task not done
when 'twas done, as well it may have seemed to some;
well-snug in a stragglers' drawing room —
drawing more crowds to the fold, more than mere blood
though mere money meant merely some uninvented hell.
To some. To some small knave chewing at the cud —
no biting at the bit for her. At the brink of her own ink well

the waves swell sail-swung at the feet of her shut-eyed twin,
akin on the thin red wall. How small a body to subpoena
them all. How thin a thing to suit gaol Moll-kindly,

when the great Dane dies over again
on the cold-contoured bathtub-riverbed.
At least spleen-venting bent over backwards for every paid
mouth, each lawyer bartering his southernness for sin,
each lecher selling mother outright for a bid in which to win her

own daughter. Own lock-rape. Take another drink,
more opium balm. Teach me how to leave
with the one-another's living, how to sack me from singing
and shut-up-shop from the bank. (River/money/verb).
Leave word with the gaoler: take no bribes — libel links
us together. Learn to own water. Discern not to sink, heave
heart upwards, give conditionally. Elope only to exact escape,
keep lovers simple and sweet. Sweat only song, and sing only sleep.

These are Not Our Stories

Who will give you a character —
in this labyrinth of cilia;

the left ventricle of the heart
with its apex cavity filled

with two bodies as the river
gives up its dead.

Dura Mater and pia mater,
coagulum in the senate.

Criminal conversation
became congress and took itself

to be seen to. Took place by force
of sheer will.

The echoes from the clubs
would have it she was

taken up tenderly and swift
to be hurled from the nearest bridge.

There's a shorthand for that:
sartorial vice has metonymic limits

cocked into a featured cap
and starving.

Who will give you a name
for your maiden form?

Is your child heathy and
is it a child of colour?

A cutter and a ketch
burial at Earl's Court.

See the sagittal section
through to the maxilla

eaten by fish, souterrain
holistically healed

by femoral aortic aneurysms,
this anatomical crucifixion

feeds a fiction, the skin
of Marsus and St Bart's.

This hand work is hard work
to dispense with; thou art sequestra,

articulate bone distractor —
stitches false as idols.

The catlin moves with ease
through the floors and seas,

finds Calvaria proximal and distal,
hunting its ground

like a pistol. Who made you thus?
Remember well

what the room looks like,
welt-full of wit and smoulder:

harmony, ice age resistance —
though these are not our stories to tell.

Forensic Artistry

Make a clean beast of it.
The tyranny of the body
in easy speeches, its winds utopia
and groove is in the heart of the

beholder. Mighty ketone erotic,
finders law and order,
intensely, is

form expunges itself daily
over breakfast of locust
meat: what is its ultimate aim if

only to promulgate the necessary?
Couldn't find the centrepiece
for these tokophobic teeth. Why

miss it when if all is held epidural
feeds itself this whole pattern?
Wonderful arena of pursed lips

why not feel it

limit under epidermal
weight as much as
much allows.

Rapier Wit

Lamentable wounds and slaughters, tabula rasa.
Water gods grin and grimace, the rope of metallurgy.
In need-fires are needle hay, workable treasures;
an exercise in *murrain* on rough terrain.

High art and lethal purpose, ultra marine,
mysterious floor plans. Tybalt gurns
in his enamelled recesses, a Dutch fencing
manual warms his haunches

with wildfire. Ottoman enemies will swamp deadlier,
more murderous Dresden and Saxony
while quillions buckle in vermillion
comfort. Plucked pauldron, fashionable accoutrements,

razed *ropera*: the sword of the robe in vulpine
clothing. Grieve and greave must, our
neatsfoot oil demands it. Raise your planishing
hammer, strike gold in interlocking crystals.

Come Beltane, instant marquetry, invisible
macula. No girls allowed, except at the hill foot.
Cross-hatched camaraderie is heat-blued and swept-hilt
harquebusier; light cavalry only, cuirassier counterfeit

and scimitar. Feel one's way with a parrying dagger:

false damascening masks and fine foliate scrolls.
Mannerist inventions dictate engrailed lines
Auto-da-fé, baluster turned. Will Lammas bring

its cinquedea while crop fronts fail en masse;
relief ornament, love fuller garniture
gives its last in miniature movements:
a Christian warrior reads: the rapier debased

swordsmanship by applying science to the equation,
reaps a tempered martensite and mail coats are pearlite,
tasset, gauntlet. Only steel hardens as quenching
the principle of negative space.

Alchemy / The Spirit and Extent of Madness

There's a goldmine in going to war
in different guises,
filching a hopeful gulf in handguns
and fleur-de-lys. She

kept house for Rumplestiltskin,
gnawed Republican humour. Searching
kempt and ridiculed doorways for
the sequestered girl who kept

her mousquetaire half-buttoned,
tap-toed and kneejerk in jest;

the veritable mirror of imbeciles.
A vapour in spin and nectar-wringing,
annul it; half moon of a Byron-gloved
hand. Wince it full, and wish it bone idol.

An uncanny ability: turning substance
— meaning moribund meat — into
accidents — meaning pure, slurry
symbols; neat, incurred and asked for,

her hair like Pardoner's straw, unspun,
Rapunzel's trousseau tried and worn.

The Economies of William Herbert Sheldon

Everyone is us, our Berliner-half extends to unlikely latitudes, our
        lives
depend upon slag and silt fodder farther than one may think.

Think of our pens as an anti-retroviral syringe loaded with the one
        thing
we cannot trust. This is why the branch fattens edifice, our lifeblood

sweet sucked vampirically over the seductive stroke of the photo-
copier — its unending capacity for franking — while each day

the hurt swells electric pools into the fretted office, feted for
fallout sometime in the next financial year.

Why every extremity lengthens its arms and tightens its belly
        against surplus
disarms me; muscle-flex the pay cheque against the ever-evident
        mercenary,

here is an accursed match for levity. The endomorphic worker
        sucks her guns,
her lunchbreak in the back of a broom-cupboard subsidised by
        anorexic

marketing amassed within a controlled environment: confirmation
        of entropy.

Carry me home one stratum away from review, strut stiletto
        anxiety

disguised when mesomorphic rants are refuse itself;
refused inappropriate entry into retainable public policy.

Anglo-American fiction, miraculous coinage when one contends its
        nothings
over feasts, beasts and blue-eyed boys.

Once more for the cheap seats in the staffroom; several tidied-up
recyclings later when the ectomorphs' impure health is fated for
        injury,

agenda offending sales targets as weaponry. Wake us up next
        spring:
we'll forsake our leisure time for your overtime, choke us up

resplendent rhetoric over coffee and load that syringe with honey,
the ultimate shock placebo in a wet-thighed appraisal economy.

Wunderkammer

Triptych:
one man asks where birds are flying,
one asks where they've flown,
one states the fact

only as a perfect
parliament of vowels.

Francis Bacon blurs his head,
a focused line too capitalist in nature;

Amanda Palmer's perfect approach
to crowdfunding.

Wonder where they'll be
in monarchy terms, stuck in

the corner with the mock crocs
confiscated from customs —

dallying another baby like
a parasol fed its own

formula and milking it, masking
its unenviable right to suck.

The Black Lodge and the White

Ghosts are the vital energy of histories that we ignore or suppress, within ourselves and within society. They are a protest and a resistance. They are a survival that asks us to look for what we're missing, what we refuse to (learn to) see.

SOPHIE MAYER, 'GHOST'

Fit the shoe at any riven point.
Ekphrasis gives and guts
as its dancer cuts and dies.

Moira should know better, really,
carbon bent by Kate. Whooping unilaterally
in these mega-soft tercets.

Give in to the shy smiles and iron curtains,
literally velvet. Hold it up for the Maria Schneider
situation. If faced with a Marlon,

who would not cast the first stone-faced
cinema. Rivas are waves and who cares
who knows it. Put down

a unionised foot and crush
the man's ultimate satin;
only does it because he knows

its elaborate nothing. Melts with it,

utterly into a momentous piece
of work. Well done, Sir. Riches,

surely. What if Bertolucci
wrapped his virgin-pushing
producers round the Russian

folktales, removed her toe by sole
over bended knee, masked
by mad love axed on opening night

tongue ripped Oppenheimer
raking it all in those bloody red shoes
ankle laid on thigh bones

like homing pigeons, chopping
the wood like a nemesis.
Those lumbersexual moments —

intimacies carved onto pestles,
Marlene Dietrich's lampblack
crushed into castor, macerating

gum arabic, as always, wisely.
Miraculous wet chemistry.
Leaden fashion, momentous medicine,

Mortar shot and boardroom
stranglers, faux and shocked

in intermediary custom, cultural

relative chasm, hold up half
the sky without qualms:
can you do it? Pharma push the in
betweens. The queen is hoping herself,
loping over the princess indulged
in a spot of well-oiled Indian exotica

within red velvet or blue. Cut a
bobsleigh; cut the colours. It's all such
sweet, cut glass erotica.

III

DISSENT

I'm a gasoline gut with a vaseline mind but
Wanna disco? Wanna see me disco?
Let me hear you depoliticize my rhyme
One! Two! Three! Four!
You got what you been asking for
You're so policy free and your fantasy wheels
And everything you think
And everything you feel is
Alright, alright, alright, alright, alright

LE TIGRE, DECEPTACON

With a Small ©

Pronouns duped by statute
how would they hurt if barbed

with all our synchronicities
tarred and feathered.

We wondered if
sharing worked much harder

in ages of empire.
They did until the drones

arrived, heat-sapped
and warranted out

for pastoral realities, our
intellectual properties

backed and wrenched.
Patent participles past

caring. We dip-dyed them
outside the justice arch

of the back bench.
He said she said that she

wasn't right and needed wasting.
Counselled with civil procedure

all the chancery counts, their wares,
their very trademark chancing it

and rightly proper. Cities
bend to their gender,

a solemn indisputable
surrender absconds

its private recusants
and reprobate system.

Privy Counsel

And think out the clink in the armoury
think: might it unsheath Carmelite
novices in the broad gardens —

who can con missile crises
only for monstrous Alsatia,

seek sanctuary in the Whitefriars grounds,
hang up Manx stockings
on a marble mantelpiece.

You can hear the Temple Bar
folding its arms over a masterpiece
of a sermon.

Just where the buck stops
fast against the kingly wall
melt one's freedoms; here
the doctor paid the hack,

hoping hard for a sell
block under axe, the English way,
united in bleeding menace

foaming at the writ, be done
with it; pillars of the earth

can't touch this watery summons.

Ill met by Fleet Street,
prisms prised the pain
away from honour

of judgment, manifest wisdom,
my soul's leech, well meant
the Minories, the Mint, unpalatable
acts of parliament.

Virgo / Virago

Have a gavel in here somewhere if you try
hard enough. Hurting glory holes like a mad hatter.

Discipline your graces.

Tassi answered: A marriage was being negotiated
between the said Artemisia and that *modenese*
who was keeping her. And I was the mediator,

who knew.

Since I dealt with both parties, and thus
I negotiated the marriage; said, as in "marriage"
with *modnese* because I was asked to do so.

By Gentileschi.

And the reason it didn't come about
was that the said young man

told me that he had
very good information

that Artemisia was a whore.

And I was an impromptu testator.

I have nothing to declare but my genius.

But they always believed me
as if I had blue eyes.

Especially holding a toothpick
to a torturer; I held impressive peace;

not mine: neither truth
nor peace, mind you.

Mattify the unabiding falsehood;
begun to be spun with strange chimeras
into macho masonry.

Held forth hardly. Bear it down;
it carts its monthly tricks.

Shun it hard and hug
your nearest testatrix.

Inviolate

'When people like Elliot can go into a store and buy a gun that makes America less safe. I'm not anti-gun, I own guns myself but this is ridiculous. People like this should not be able to own guns.' HOLLYWOOD SCREENWRITER DALE LAUNER

Stay course. Fold over again.
Stand back on coarse modes.
He's singing again.

Please refrain, pull wool over.
Hard graft contains 'him',
pulls pronouns towards the dark star.

Dispense with them. Higgs boson
vitiates that language may intervene,
so 'God' discerns as damning youth

fastens fatal, 'she' may collapse.
It's as if those banks are braes, condensed;
trading arms for tenure.

There's time to be meek,
to inherit the earth that way
and speak for 'him' who

speaks for us. How awkward in fact,
in childhood; one or another will list

how 'he' cannot form fists

yet learnt to play in html.
Choose words like 'simmering'
or 'seething'; or cockney-rhyming

runt of the litter. 'He' shouldn't have guns.
Should be a psych test for that,
the 9mm question semi-automatic;

of course it's constitutionally heavy:
libations of weaponry wield full crux
over methodology, ideology.

Lacking something literate here.
Need magazines for mentioning yet again,
how so few have future names;

further proof that London
culture owes us words and witnesses
and probably mistresses.

Oh to be so dispossessed,
Alpha diazepam disowns you ironically.
He's talking over it but clinically.

Are there words for the wastrels, then.
Hassle your shares,
model your wares, there's

hunger in production, sisters.
Solder sorority out of
air miles, American expression,

or put in a box with Marinetti's
manifest destiny any chance of moderate pain,
or voluntary gain. Put on a silencer:

rescind vocal rights; general debunk.
Leave 'his' pronoun leaning and pining
and lyrically void and blank.

Phobos Anomaly

'You're a marine, one of Earth's toughest, hardened in combat and trained for action. Three years ago you assaulted a superior officer for ordering his soldiers to fire upon civilians. He and his body cast were shipped to Pearl Harbor, while you were transferred to Mars, home of the Union Aerospace Corporation.

The UAC is a multi-planetary conglomerate with radioactive waste facilities on Mars and its two moons, Phobos and Deimos. With no action for fifty million miles, your day consisted of suckin' dust and watchin' restricted flicks in the rec room.' THE DOOM MANUAL, ID SOFTWARE, 1993.

A man walks into a death lab, doesn't flinch.
And every inch is steel rule, 'pure gasoline',
mitochondrial defects taped up

to hair peace. Arch into abandonware,
crack-based wanton man, no reader;
being the last alive means no road movie,

who only read the book. It's a red, dead
thing who only stand and wait, but once
dead the beasts burden themselves as a lover

and move towards a third gestation. This
one's a station commander, a blinder of
a fellow. Official reports reveal toy stories,

tin soldiers have their heads rearranged
academically, their molten rush combustible
to the mermaids whose transports spun

one cup of DDT into heady green
raunch. Machine gun hymn slam to
blunderbuss, rocket launcher distorts,

loved a little lurker, went all out
for some intergalactic Hemingway
in the war-torn heart where home heaves

a warning; passed on gets and burnished nets
while star ship troopers stropped their last
over muscular marked dimensions.

Here, indentured demon dentistry runs
hard and fast in the rude red cross
with a blister pack of codeine. Rare first aid

trips and schemes, amends the strip of tree,
the field of streams, those gaping ragged
jaw lines and callisthenic marines.

Inverse Alcaic

Leer, my master; by day fools fearless lechers,
kind behind your square of glass. Night, and doors dance
into hinges, kisses fumble down
towards flinches. Children, not sleeping, chant

murmurs, tales, so as not to hear those lung-gnarled alms
cast the first stone and the last. Bruised, the fawn-like
eyes lie darkly on the frame, lie still:
though beaten and clinging are token cant.

Chasseresse

Rarity, porphyria and is the blood eagle real.

Satin, petri and petty, cash me out. Statins ferment

intermittently, currying kingly demons.

A bitch called quarantine.

Querelles des femmes,

Enter Hippocrates and Galen,

feigning fortitude in worthy-making hypocrisies;

non-entities with wombs tender resignations —

always negotiate. There was no purple pigment.

There are always skaldic forums,

scathing the mud from the bone,

teasing cartilage across mucus membranes

like osmosis in reverse.

He said the blood went to my brain

and of course it was madness

to leave the house.

I left him then, paring hang nails

with a hunter's knife,

collapsed the butcher's block

unstopped by moonlight

and various capricious tides –

locked myself in an operating theatre,

holding fort like a man: mad, madam,

pitching my tools just right.

Under Gloss

First place anyway it flirts with neglect and its accompanying
       –isms,
change the odds don't like them. Even in myrrhical rich
       surveillances,
gold compasses transfer like a good girl, wildly manning the many
preponderances of is this a legal file-share, when all the baby wants
       to do is
suckle opprobrium through heat, replete with a frank sense of
       nurture.

Many a time the board refused, to undo is to be undone,
and is to look upon ye mighty works is to be salted into submission.
and when will we ask the super cipher question what
if a humming child was draped upon the lichen,
what if its human heart was sectioned 28 minutes

to the millimetre, fancying only its undue discourse and
many times severed its course. Its ictus ricocheted into its
only temperamental disclosure, if I could have told the mischief
of this, so many lives would have been that much worth the
       opening.
why every time her mouth opens it unders, as if her second

breast gives over manly measures, second-guessing how much
gullet can be deciphered via reading, bending force-over-tongue
in glottal scraping; scandal orating scoundrel how many lushes

rush in every second week. So boring the elaborate taxonomy
of the Crumb family, that bed of nails apposite to continuing

to self-abuse through pointillism, *stripping the jeans off of* every
decent woman with decent timing. Metronomic zippers
beat morphine every time. How perfectly goddamned delightful
it all is, to be sure; see crumby bait in scribbles, that multi-hating
mother makes her mark every humble second, meets her makers.

Pilgrims

What manner are we
of manor born into rust?
Marx its members' tusks.

Hold the front page, lass.
Waugh's words have a halting mass;
irate and press pass.

Make face with feeling;
there's healing in seeming shy,
high and whisky dry.

Take home the drinks kit.
We bit off more to chew with
Cachaça than most.

All noise, embrace it,
even if Backstreet Boys sound
strangely like NSYNC.

Sleepyheads of the
cruel world personified
in Monday mornings.

Hope for Waterworld.
Drum it up with nail and I

always hope for more.

What happens when all
rancours under the arras?
Does Hamlet forget?

Langland, idiot
he is, left his passport tight
in verse four, edit.

Leonard Cohen must
be obeyed, so fade/dance me
to the end of love.

Count your money, just
to see if silence missed it
trying to shut mouths.

While commissioned, kiss
constituent parts; its hearts
all construe themselves.

This Wolf Comes in 3D

These walls come in 3D and everything else, and this is ground-
        breaking —
even in 1992. Even after the Doom manual landed, pseudo-Nazis
        hold sway.
This is not a state to be drunk in, or to vote in.

The old blood in the new order, even these words in this order. The
        phoenix
from the ashes of Joy Division. Sitting there ruefully
wondering what happened to dignity.

When all is played and won, a last laugh is worth something in a
querulous face-off, literally: the secret wall gave me a nose bleed,
        tripping over keys.
Searching for coordinates in Castle Wolfenstein,

I feel immersed, exported like Heineken.
That waking world is sparse and gorgeous, if gory as spilt milk.
It's a world that says that I am great and semi-digital. That piercing
        extra body parts

is a valid method of self-expression: if one can't buy mutilation one
        is silenced,
a brittle member. One is divested of their *ausweis*. Get psyched,
        spear of destiny.
Give it a blast of its Versailles-dug grave-feed. This is an

exploitation movie

penned by Sarah Kane, arraigned in blood and hecatombs.
Horses here are really mules in Emperors' clothing and Hitler has a
    Gatling gun.
He melts on point of contact and dribbles hyperlipids

into guttersnipers. His likeness is everywhere and players bear an
    unheimlich
resemblance to Pac-Man: faceless and hungry. This commander is
    keener
than most, his upper lip hirsute in brackets and chemical warfare.

Mengele would approve of this pastime. You now have broken
thumbs and your hell sings of enemy territory. Even the limbs are a
tessellation of swastikas, a *dies irae* for the unrestrained, unjilted
    generation.

Bloodwork

Half-meant by second readings,
and hell-bent on structure;
this Sodom's lot's a deuteronomy of infra-
red. That said the wife

shall prick her finger on a spinning wheel and meet
the beat behind the bloodlust;
O peak of a changed changed heart,
the mark of a thrifty maker.

Many-seizéd scalpel, the scalene,
untouched privacy of nursing
a throatful of saline;
kneel and tire of

love not lightly given.
When the hungry cannot
feed, I see heartening in
the bloody sap of a knife

edge, meaning bleed in hungry
rhythms; needing, instead,
the frank trust impeded by
thirty-second phone calls

and every pleasure mastered.

To think: what sense is this
that feeds on sulphur,
melding feats of cinder belts

and making dark the duels?
I can hear this multiple
schism flinch in sync
with the snap of synapse;

your breathing and blood
will be simple and thus:
waiting for soft rocks to harden
to salve your inevitable carbon.